REAL SAFE DEFENSE

Safety, Defense, & Survival Strategies for Busy Real Estate Professionals!

by

Edward T. Aiken

DEDICATION

I would like to dedicate this book to all of the hard-working Real Estate Professionals who risk it everyday.

CONTENTS

Acknowledgments   i

1   Safety, Awareness, &   Pg 10
    Doing Your Job

2   Thank You Facebook,   Pg 24
    You Are Very
    Informative

3   Things You can   Pg 35
    Implement Right Away
    to Keep You Safe

4   Do Smartphones Really   Pg 47
    Make Us Smarter

5   Spatial Awareness is   Pg 61
    Critical

6   Starting with Your Fight   Pg 76
    & Flight Plan

7   Setting Up For Survival   Pg 84

8   The Skinny on   Pg 95
    Experiencing Violence
    While on the Job

9   Guns, Knives, Pepper   Pg 103
    Spray...Oh My

10   The Tactical Pen A   Pg 115
    Realtor's Best Friend

ACKNOWLEDGMENTS

I would like to acknowledge the following people with which this book would not have been possible...

To My Past & Present Teachers, Students, and Fellow Martial Artists...

You are an Inspiration.

To my Friends & Family...

You are the Best a man could get stuck with.

And Finally to my Beautiful Wife...

I Love You Fantastically!

INTRODUCTION

Welcome and Thank You for reading REAL SAFE DEFENSE. This book is for those Real Estate Professionals who are aware of the potential dangers that Real Estate Agents face while on the job and take it seriously enough to want to do something to improve their own safety. If that sounds like you then by all means keep reading.

I know your time is valuable so allow me to take the time now to assure you that this information is absolutely worth it.

Briefly I'd like to give you some background on myself so you know who I am and why I am qualified to write on this subject.

My name is Ed Aiken and I am currently a Certified Real Estate Appraiser and Professional Martial Arts Instructor. I have over 20 years experience in Real Estate and over 35 years experience in Self Defense and the Martial Arts and I have put this book together for you based on my experiences in those fields.

In the past, I have been a Buyers Agent, a Sellers Agent, a Loan Officer, Loan Processor, an Investor, and a Real Estate Appraiser (which I am still currently). I have taught, supervised, and trained over 50 appraiser trainees and have managed, taught, and trained a dozen or so real estate agents and loan officers.

As far as my Martial Arts background goes I have had the opportunity to train with some of the Best of the Best in their fields (One of my instructors was the exclusive hand to hand trainer for SEAL Team 6 out of Virginia Beach).

I am a Full Instructor in Jeet Kune Do Concepts and am also a 1st Degree Black Belt in Brazilian Jiu Jitsu. I have trained with over 40 instructors in various arts and have coached, taught, and mentored individuals and professional fighters for many years.

I don't tell you any of this to impress you but

to impress upon you that the information I have for you is the absolute best available in regards to Safety, Defense, and Survival when it comes to being a Real Estate Agent/Professional.

You may or may not have ever run into a 'problem' while showing new clients a house, meeting a new client at a vacant property, or sitting alone at an open house. Hopefully you never will. Chances are if you've been in the industry for any length of time, you know someone personally or have heard of someone who has had a problem.

And if you haven't that's fine, I promise you will be better off knowing what I am going to share with you than not.

Years ago, I got my start in Real Estate by working at a very busy Residential Appraisal Office in Los Angeles. I started part time as an office assistant, but before I knew it they had me get my Trainees License. They were so busy that they needed me to go out and inspect properties.

So with a little prodding, I got my license and within a couple days of receiving it, I was out looking at 8-12 properties a day...by myself!

Talk about learning in the trenches!

It was tough and in order to keep up with my workload I was forced to develop a system to make sure I could do everything. I needed to inspect the properties, take the comp photos, and make it to my next appointment on time while battling with L.A. Traffic!

It wasn't unheard of that I would drive to Long Beach, then up to Hollywood, then down to Manhattan Beach, then back up to Hollywood, then all the way down to Orange County...in one day!

I worked all over...including some pretty high crime areas like East L.A., Compton, and Watts.

Well on one particular day I had an appointment in a bad part of Compton. Compton is actually much nicer nowadays but back then there were some pretty sketchy areas. I didn't really worry too much about it at the time but I do admit I did my inspections a little 'faster' when I was in those areas.

Anyway...the house I was looking at was vacant, so I got out of the car and started right away. As the first part of my system I would measure the house and take the exterior photos as I went along. Once I was done with the outside, I would then move onto the next part of my system which was to inspect the interior and take photos of the inside.

Well, because I had this system I did every house in practically the same manner.

I would walk in the front door and then move very quickly through the house in a counter clockwise fashion (don't ask me why), going from room to room.

Now in this particular house, before I knew it, I found myself rounding the corner to the second bedroom towards the back of the house. I'll never forget what happened next.

As I turned the corner to the room there was a guy crouched in the corner near the closet.

Now...needless to say this guy scared the Bejeezus out of me!

His eyes were wide open and dilated, he was breathing heavy, and to make matters worse he was clutching a metal pipe!

Well, at that age I was also already an accomplished martial artist and was also training pretty regularly with SEAL Team 6's instructor.

One of the first things he taught me was that

someone who has the jump on you and who is armed...has a huge advantage over you despite whether or not they have any training. It's not like the movies. One shot is all it takes. I was in a bad spot and knew it.

In fact, the moment I realized just HOW bad a spot I was in was the moment I also realized that it was about to get much worse.

I heard a noise in the next room and realized there was SOMEONE ELSE in the house as well. Really not good. Without a doubt I had to act fast.

At this point I would love to tell you that I busted out some crazy Matrix-like moves and quickly took out these 2 attackers but that's not what happened.

Instead, I assessed, judging by the crouching guy's clothing, that this guy and his friend were using the house because they were homeless. I'm sure they were on something as well but they were mainly using the house as their livings quarter more than a drug den.

I looked at the crouching guy and could tell he was somewhat scared. So, I told him in a loud voice, loud enough so that the person in the other room could hear...'Hey, I'm just an appraiser checking the structure of the house and didn't realize you were in here. It's cool if you don't mind me finishing my inspection, I don't mind you being here...it's not my house.'

After a tense few seconds, the guy smiled and called out to his friend that it was okay. He then proceeded to give me a tour of the rest of the house.

In a way I could tell he was proud of the fact that he was showing me the house. It was like he felt it was partly his. Needless to say, his jolly demeanor didn't soothe my jitters, I knew I had to stay on high alert and I made sure he and his friend stayed in front of me. I finished the inspection and left....quickly.

Now I'm of no illusion that this scenario could have turned out very, very badly. They could have attacked me, beat me, stabbed me, shot me, tied me up...who knows. Sure I could've fought, but the point is I put MYSELF in a very bad situation and almost paid for it...all because I was doing the same thing I had done day in and day out...hundreds of times before.

So, I ask you...

How often are you doing the same thing without realizing it?

Probably much more than you think.

Well that's okay because, that's what I'm here for. Together we're going to develop a Safety Plan for you. That's what this guide is for. I hope you take full advantage of our time together because you never know when you might need it.

So...let's get to it.

CHAPTER 1

SAFETY, AWARENESS, & DOING YOUR JOB!

Just over a year before the writing of this...our industry experienced a tragedy. One of our own paid the ultimate price while doing her job. A Successful Arkansas Realtor by the name of Beverly Carter was abducted from one of her showings and murdered, you probably heard about it.

My heart goes out to her friends and family and if anything good can come from something so tragic perhaps it is in the awareness of you knowing, through Beverly's example, what can actually happen to you while doing your job and finding out what you can do personally to ensure that something like that doesn't repeat.

So let's talk about Safety Awareness and doing your job.

For the most part, I think nowadays real estate offices provide their agents with at least a printout of safety guidelines which they should follow and some training. Perhaps your office has it's own safety guidelines. That's good because it wasn't always like that.

I know many real estate offices follow the Guidelines and Recommendations of the National Association of Realtors. In fact, I would say that the NAR has probably done the most of any organization to help agents prepare for potentially dangerous situations. I know that they are releasing a new safety program sometime later this year and I have to think that the Beverly Carter murder was a big impetus for that to come about.

The more resources for safety we have...the better.

The NAR even recommends to offices that they offer a variety of safety AND self defense training to suit the different personalities and preferences of the agents. They realized that that Self Defense is an important part of your overall safety but also that your preference of Self-Defense might be different. Not everyone wants to carry a gun, or pepper spray.

The fact is you are faced with a lot of choices and Self Defense options. Through this guide I am going to help you to navigate through it.

The first thing to know is that there is no one answer when it comes to Self Defense. The lesson here I want you to get is to never fall into the trap that you believe you have enough when it comes to your own Safety, Defense, and Survival. It requires continual awareness and frequent training.

Sure you don't have to do it all the time but you do need to practice it periodically. Think of it like it's the continuing education you need to maintain your real estate license, only this is to maintain your personal safety (something much more valuable in the long run).

I actually do believe we should have required continuing education for self-defense because we are in a higher risk job sector. Not to mention also...

We are creatures of habit...

We have to do what we can to keep on top of our business while at the same time making sure we are not indulging in habits that can hurt us fiscally or physically! It's a lot to balance and can be hard to determine what to do when it comes to your safety versus your clients needs.

When analyzing what happened to Beverly, the consensus amongst her peers is that prior to her abduction...she did a lot right as far as her safety was concerned and her business. She was very successful and took the precautions that she was taught.

On that fateful night, Beverly phoned her husband and let him know where and who she would be meeting. In fact this is how the police identified the subject so quickly. I know there are some reports that she was meeting a new client and didn't know him but I do believe she at least had his name and some information on the guy.

Beverly no doubt had a routine that had some safety guidelines in place. Upon arriving at the house that night, she left her purse and wallet in the car. This is often taught to Realtors so as not to tempt a potential threat into attacking them and taking their purse. Beverly knew this...

Now...most training that you will receive from your office will go on to tell you some other things to do to be safe, but to be honest, almost all fail to offer details of what you should do should an actual attack happen.

My feeling is that the reason for this is that most people coming up with the office safety guidelines are doing so from the perspective of avoidance. In other words...if they employ the strategy of avoidance, bad things won't happen. There's of course, a problem with this...

The problem isn't actually with using an avoidance strategy but in that the people preaching avoidance have only had to USE avoidance to keep safe. They have no experience with actual violence. They have never trained nor studied nor actually experienced real violence themselves. The fact is, bad things can and do happen no matter how much you try to avoid them and you need to know what to do if it happens to you.

Unfortunately, I don't think Beverly ever got THAT kind of training.

When you truly consider your Safety, you have to base it on the assumption that the worst things possible are going to happen. Many so-called safety experts don't study how violence actually occurs because they don't come from this perspective.

They don't know how violent encounters-abductions, assaults, robberies, rape, etc., really transpire. They don't actually study the physical effectiveness of pepper spray, hand guns, or various modes of empty hands self defense.

So...they don't know to teach their agents certain things like when the most likely time it is that a Realtor is going to be attacked or how to respond.

In case you are wondering...that time is upon or just before/after entering or exiting the house. I can't help to feel that knowing this one fact could have helped Beverly.

Here's a quote from the Arkansas News regarding Beverly Carter's Abduction. 'Beverly's husband knew something was wrong when he went to the house she was showing. Her truck was parked in the driveway with her purse and wallet inside, and the door to the house was wide open'.

Now...I'm not saying 100% that Beverly was abducted when she was going in the house or when she was exiting but it's pretty likely given the door was open. And even if something else happened like he grabbed her inside and knocked her out then carried her to a waiting car without being able to close the door; that's fine...but when it comes to developing a realistic safety program we've got to look at the statistics and experiences of agents who have actually been victimized while on the job as well as how violence actually occurs in these instances.

Take the case of a San Antonio agent by the name of Janice Tisdale...

Janice got the call from a known client and agreed to meet him at a vacant house. Her client had previously portrayed himself as a wealthy businessman and she had shown him several high end homes in the past.   This time he managed to use her trust and lure her to a vacant multimillion dollar house.

Although she had met him several times beforehand, Janice said she still felt something wasn't quite right. Her so-called client was acting strange. To her credit, she too left her jewelry and purse in the car just like Beverly did.

When the client's banker didn't show up with the client as he said he would, she started having second thoughts about doing the showing. Despite her intuition she agreed to do the showing anyway. When she bent over to grab the lock box, he struck her on the head with a metal bar.

Luckily, Janice survived and ended up getting away after being held for 45 minutes but the point of this is the point at which he decided to attack her. He chose the moment she bent over to get the lock box because she was in a vulnerable position and was distracted. Had she known this is the most likely time an attacker will strike, she might have listened to her intuition and saved herself some stitches.

I don't mean to make light of her situation or how she handled it. Janice was a flight attendant and was trained to remain calm in the face of adversity but my point is that the more realistic information available to you...the better.

A perpetrator looks for victims/targets of opportunity. A female real estate agent at a vacant house who is momentarily distracted is the perfect opportunity. Criminals will use the moment when they are least likely to get resistance to make their move. If you know this...you can be ready and mitigate their attack.

Now...just as I said most safety experts don't know how actual violence occurs AND most defense experts not only don't know how to realistically prepare you for actual violence, but they don't know how you actually need to do your job while staying safe at the same time.

Consider this...I recently read that Janice no longer goes to houses alone and always carries a gun. This is a good strategy. I am a big advocate for concealed carry as long as the carrier has the proper training with a handgun and that usually means that they have to get hours of supplemental training.

What I mean by that is that a handgun can give you a false sense of security. I'm sure a well meaning Self Defense or Handgun Instructor taught Janice some things after her experience. Hopefully, it is good information.

Let's imagine if Janice was already a gun carrier at the time of her attack and Janice had not left her purse in the car but instead carried it with her because she had her gun in it...do you think it would have made a difference when her supposed client attacked her?

Most likely the answer is no given the time the guy attacked her. Remember she would've had to deploy (retrieve) the gun from her purse before she could use it and this guy waited until she was distracted and then hit her. If she didn't have her hand on the gun and/or had it out already it would do her little good as she wouldn't have had time to react. Remember my instructor's lesson on when a person has the jump on you.

These are things that you have to think about and train. Having your hand in your pocket or in a purse the wrong way might tip off your attacker that you have a weapon or may cost you a client in the event they are legit. Remember we've got to balance our safety with our business.

Unfortunately most defense instructors don't cover things like this because they don't take into consideration how you need to do your job. They just think you can grab your gun any old time or just carry it around with you in your hand as you're showing a newlywed couple their first house.

Of course there are ways to modify things for how you have to do your job.

For example, Janice, when she was getting the key from the lock box, could have bent down with her hand in her purse like she was getting the supra key out of it when really she was touching her gun. This way Janice could then effectively respond if her attacker made a move to strike her while she is opening the door. She easily could fire while the gun is in the purse or pull it out if she has the distance and freeze him in his tracks. This of course takes a little training to become second nature but not all that much.

When it comes to your personal safety you have to constantly analyze your routines...how you are doing things, and how things are likely to occur. You've got to match how to best do your job and still be safe. It wouldn't be very good business to follow around your buyers as you show them a house all the while you have one hand on the gun in your waistband or purse. You probably wouldn't keep clients very long. No...you've got to find the happy medium.

The best safety strategies are the ones that allow you to continue doing business effectively while at the same time ensuring you can still go home at night. We often will sacrifice our safety unknowingly to satisfy our clients. That's never a good thing. Even worse is when we think we have taken enough steps to prepare ourselves for violence only to realize that we've done too little too late.

Personally, I'm a middle man. I want to be

safe AND successful and hopefully you do too. As one of my instructors taught me...the objective is to take your body home with you at night so you can enjoy all the nice things you've acquired.

Hopefully, you're starting to think of your own Safety & Awareness Plan with a Realistic Slant...for that is the point of this chapter. Now let's move on.

If you would like more Resources on Safety, Defense, and Survival...go to www.RealSafeDefense.com.

CHAPTER 2

THANK YOU FACEBOOK...YOU ARE VERY INFORMATIVE!

Ahh...the Information Age. How you have made the previously unknown...Known. Now I KNOW what you're thinking. You think that I am going to lecture you on divulging too much personal information on a public forum like Facebook while simultaneously thinking that I don't realize how important social networking is to your business.

Well...to be honest, whether you use Facebook or not for personal or business use doesn't matter to me. I think to be competitive today, social networks are a necessity. What matters to me more is how aware you are of the craftiness of the criminals out there who might use your info for nefarious means.

It's no secret that when it comes to physical violence, most attackers know their victims. In fact, in the Beverly Carter murder there are currently a husband and wife who have been charged with her abduction, kidnapping, and murder.

It has been reported that the wife knew Beverly because her daughter and Beverly's granddaughter were in the same cheer leading program together.

No it wasn't a Facebook connection but I ask this...What Info If Any did the Suspects gain from Facebook and How Did They Use It?

Here's a scenario I want you to think about. Imagine you are a person with less than good intentions. You meet someone at your daughter's cheer leading event. You see that they are driving a nice car and wearing nice clothes. You ask your child what the girl's name is who is with the nice lady driving the nice car. She of course tells you.

You go back home and put the child's name into Facebook and low and behold one of her relatives has made a facebook page for her. You click on it...search through her friends (since it's not a private page), and you find the lady who 'you are curious about'.

Now you look on her profile and see that she works for ABC Realty.

You Google ABC Realty and her name and find out her number, her open houses schedule, that she likes to ride horses on the weekend, and that she is successful.

All of this takes less than 5 minutes. Thanks Zuckerburg. You have taken all the effort out of stalking.

Now here's another scenario I want you to consider only this time from your own perspective.

The phone rings and it's someone looking at and ready to buy an 800k+ house that you are familiar with. Now this isn't just someone. This is Joey from the block...Rita's block. Joey knows your good friend Rita who happens to be in Mexico btw. Joey knows Rita because they used to ski together at Aspen when they were in their

20's. You vaguely remember Rita talking about skiing in Aspen.

Joey recently spoke to Rita about his moving and before she went to Mexico on her honeymoon, Rita suggested you as an agent. Joey of course is moving to your area soon and is in a hurry to get a place. He's recently found out he is going to transfer here for work and is actually in town for the evening. His wife called him and found a place online. She is super-excited and wants Joey to look at it before his flight in the morning so they can put an all cash offer on it immediately. Joey isn't picky and really is looking at the house as a formality for his wife. As far as he's concerned if it has a roof...he'll take it.

Do you think you could meet him there in the next hour or so to show him the house?

It's vacant and has a lock box..

Now reading this I know you're probably saying, I would never fall for that but really consider it.

This guy knows your friend and knows she is on her honeymoon. You know she used to ski in Aspen and he sounds friendly. It's an all cash/relocation offer and an 800k+ house. That's a commission of $20K.

When it comes to sales think of all the primal drivers that Joey is hitting. *Trust* - he knows your friend. *Pride* - Rita recommended you. You always looked up to Rita. *Greed* - 20k is a good payday. *Scarcity/Urgency* - he's only here for 1 night then he is leaving. *Simplicity* - All Cash/Relocation...this deal is a no-brainer.

Remember the wealthy businessman that hit poor Janice on the head? Turns out he was a truck driver. It's easy to portray yourself as something you're not.

Primal drivers can blind us to 'Primal Truck Drivers'!

I know, bad pun, but I couldn't resist.

So what's the point of all this?

We all already know that Facebook/Social Info can be dangerous...

The real point is to never let your guard down and to start thinking how someone can really use information that's readily available to anyone in this day and age.

I'm not saying to be stand-offish to your clients. That would negatively impact your business. Simply, keep your awareness as often as you can. Understand when you might be in jeopardy and open to attack and don't get too comfortable around people just because you have met with them previously or they came from a referral.

Remember just because someone says they know Rita, it doesn't mean they are who they say they are...

This person may or may not be the Real Joey...but even that doesn't matter. Think about it.

Even if they were a lifelong, childhood friend of Rita...

That doesn't mean they aren't a Serial Killer as well! Dexter's sister didn't have any idea he was a Serial Killer for most of her life and she was a cop! I know...TV reference but the lesson is still valid.

Think about it, if you've ever listened to anyone who has ever known a serial killer in real life, they almost are always surprised to find out that their neighbor has been 'getting rid' of people in their basement all the while they have lived next to them borrowing their 'sugar'.

You hear quotes like...'He was always a nice boy, watering his plants and such. He would even help me with my groceries. I never in a million years would suspect he could do the things he's accused of doing.'

The unfortunate truth is that many criminals are smart and they know human tendencies and how to work them.

Not that long ago there was a crew that were robbing open houses, I think somewhere in the Greater Dallas Area. They weren't strong-arm robbing the open houses, rather they were stealing items from the houses and taking contents from the real estate agent's purses while the agents were distracted. More like stealing.

The open house crew consisted of 2 men and 1 woman. The way they would work is the woman would engage and distract the agent while the 2 men would steal valuables from the open house and take the wallets from the purse that the agent would usually leave in the kitchen.

The female suspect would usually ask the agent to show her where the bathroom was in the house and talk to her while she was 'going'. The agent's purse was being depleted by the 2 men while the client's bladder was supposedly being depleted.

This crew hit many open houses before they were caught and were very successful because they knew that most people are more likely to trust a group if a woman is part of it. Further they knew that a female agent would most likely be empathetic to the 'bathroom needs' of a fellow female.

When you think of it...this is very cunning.

Criminals are the wolves of our society and come in all shapes and sizes.

Years ago I used to work as an undercover Loss Prevention agent at a major department store. The majority of my job was to observe, follow, and detain shoplifters.

I got very good at picking out shoplifters. Yes...they often fit one of many profiles and were easy to spot once you knew what you were looking for.

But...

You would be physically shocked by the shear

variety of looks, ages, sexes, races, social-economic status, etc of the people who shoplift. There were Young Parents, Middle Age Parents, Respectable Businessmen, Businesswomen, Teenagers, Tattooed Hardened Criminals, and even Sweet Little-Old Ladies.

We learned to never be surprised by the appearance of the perpetrator and I suggest you do the same. Expect the unexpected. Trust me...you won't be paranoid, just more alert than normal.

The more you can put yourself in the shoes of these unseemly folks, the better. Imagine how easy it is nowadays to weave a story out of the digital air and you will be less likely to have the wool pulled over your eyes by one of these 'Big Bad Wolves'.

Now...on to the next lesson.

If you want more Resources on Criminal Profiling...go to www.RealSafeDefense.com.

CHAPTER 3

THINGS YOU CAN IMPLEMENT RIGHT AWAY TO KEEP YOU SAFE!

So let's get to some things you can do today to be safer.

Now...like I've said already, I've got a good amount of experience in Real Estate and I know that some of the things I am suggesting aren't always going to be practical or possible. You have a business to run and often times you've got to do things that aren't optimal for your safety in order to satisfy your client's needs and maintain your bottom line.

As long as you know that, AND you prepare

for the times when things aren't going to be optimal...you'll be just fine 99.9999% of the time.

No one can tell you you'll be safe 100% of the time and if they do they are sadly mistaken. Our job is to get as close to that 100% as possible.

Also...before we get into the actual 'What You Can Do', I've got to say that a lot of what I am going to tell you, you probably already do and/or have already heard it.

A lot of the personal safety suggestions I will be giving you are based on common sense. But, do me a favor...just because something is common sense, or you already have heard what I am suggesting...I want you to really think about whether or not you are already doing it. If you are then no worries. If not...ask yourself how you can start implementing it into your daily routine. Otherwise we're just blowing in the wind. Fair enough?

So with that said...let's move on to the first thing that you can implement tomorrow while doing your job. Bear in mind also, that these suggestions are in no particular order of importance. Anything you do that will keep you safe, no matter how small, is important.

The first thing I am going to suggest is that when possible, meet your clients in a place with lots of people, preferably your office (provided there are others there of course). Or at least have someone with you if you are meeting them elsewhere.

Once you are there, get a copy of their identification. Like I said...not always possible but it can help deter someone with bad intentions. Whether you are at your office or elsewhere, all you need to do is take a photo of their id. Just tell them it is for their file. Most people won't object since they will be handing over a good amount of their personal information in the course of buying a house.

Once you take the photo...email or text it to a 3rd party as soon as possible.

At the very least...if something does happen, and you get taken from a house, or something else happens, it can help to locate you faster and/or the perpetrator(s).

I know that's not super encouraging but every little thing counts. We will get to what to do when the shtf and things go bad a little later.

The second thing I would suggest is to never go to a vacant house or hold an open house alone. Once again, we live in the real world and have real bills to pay, so this isn't always going to be possible. Just know that the chances of violent crimes happening against you while hosting an open house will go way down when you are with another person.

But once again...just because you have someone with you it doesn't mean to let your guard down. There have been plenty of cases where multiple agents have been held up or assaulted while together.

Another thing you can do is to make sure that you do most of your appointments during daylight hours. This is kind of a double-edged sword, I'll admit. Often during the day, there are less people/neighbors around as they are usually at work, but crime statistics show that the majority of violent crimes happen at night.

Criminals prefer the cover of darkness but that doesn't mean they are confined by it.

When Janice was attacked (and Beverly too I believe), it was during daylight hours. The thing to note is that, when Janice made her move and took off, she was able to flag down some teenagers in a car. She credits them with saving her. This might not have been possible at night depending on the distance and direction the car was moving. So it's something to consider and I guarantee that most criminals know this.

So let's recap really quick...

When possible, meet with a new client first and photocopy their id. When possible, always go to a vacant house or host an open house with at least one assistant. And finally try to do most of your appointments during daylight hours.

Next thing...

For this next one I want to share a story that happened to a friend of mine. She's not a Realtor but the lesson is still relevant.

Not that long ago, a friend of mine went to meet someone to look at an item that was for sale on Craigslist. I'm actually not sure what she was buying but it required her to drive to this person's house.

When she got to the house, she parked in the driveway and went up to the door like the person told her to. On the way up to the door, a car pulled in the driveway behind her. Thinking that this was the homeowner she went over to the car.

As she approached the car a young male jumped out of the driver's side door and attempted to pull her into the car. She screamed and fought free of the guy but out of instinct she ran towards her car and got in.

The problem was she was blocked in by her attacker's car. Not a good spot to be in.

Fortunately, the Craiglist guy came to her rescue. When the attacker saw the homeowner come out the front door he took off. To her credit, she did the right thing after that and stayed in her car until the police came. Most people would've gotten out of the car and gone to the homeowner for safety.

Remember...she didn't know if he was in on it or not.

Fortunately he wasn't in on it, but he could have been. Once she felt safe and got out of the car he could have finished what the other guy had started.

So here's the point...make sure to always park your car where you won't be blocked in. I know y'all don't park where you should more than you might admit because practically every time I meet an agent at a house they pull in the driveway ahead of me.

A good rule of thumb is to show up at houses/appointments early so you can park before your clients get there and to check out the area out beforehand.

If you happen to pull up at a house at the same time as your client I would suggest you wave them in first. Just tell them you are looking for your key and to go ahead and park first.

But...even in this scenario, I personally would opt to park on a part of the street where I couldn't be blocked in. Even if you park behind them, someone else could block you in while you are inside. I know someone might be able to block you in on the street, depending on the street, but the idea is to get used to doing it as often as possible.

Remember, the goal is to take your body home with you at night so you can enjoy all the nice things you've acquired (family included). That means that the number one goal in your head, should anything go wrong, should someone attack you...is the escape safely. Where you park your car is vital to your escaping successfully.

Another thing I want to instill in you is that the overall goal isn't to fight should you get attacked. That might be part of the process that helps you to escape but that is not the goal.

The moment someone attacks you can be very shocking and you will act on instinct...this is called the Fight or Flight instinct. Whichever instinct kicks in should eventually result in you escaping safely.

If your visceral reaction in the face of danger is to take flight and you take off in a direction that boxes you in, you've only delayed the inevitable. You've effectively cornered yourself for your assailant.

If you are the type that gets mad (hence the

fight in the fight or flight response), and your natural instinct is to fight then you've got to do it with your escape in mind. Some people just go into a blind rage and start attacking without any thought of getting away. Unfortunately this doesn't always work in their favor. A strong attacker might easily overpower you despite your anger.

There are a lot of self-defense programs that will teach you to strike and strike and strike until the attacker is down for good. This isn't a terrible strategy as sometimes it is needed but I personally would rather have you strike and fight just enough so that you can escape safely. With this strategy you won't need to take the attacker out, just stun him/her enough or strike them to create enough space so you can get out of there.

Of course there are pros and cons to every approach.

Nothing is a silver bullet when it comes to your personal defense. This is why we need to do as many little things for our safety as we can. This way we can stack the odds back in our favor.

Remember, an attacker who has preplanned his/her attack has the advantage over you. We can take most of that advantage away by doing a lot of the right things but nonetheless...the attackers will always have a little more.

Since we are on the subject of Escaping...I wanted to bring up another Safety Tip.

Women (and some Men too, I'm not judging), PLEASE, PLEASE reconsider wearing high heels at work. If you have to run and you end up falling or worse breaking your ankle because you wanted to dress to impress...well, please reconsider it. My wife loves shoes (and better yet, likes to make me go with her shoe shopping), so I know there are plenty of functional yet stylish low heel shoes out there.

Here's a True Story to illustrate this point...

My wife and I just last night watched Invasion of the Body Snatchers. She had never seen it. It's an old show which I think was filmed in 1978.

Anyway, we were watching it and towards the last part of the movie, the protagonists end up running for quite some time from all the people who had become aliens.

It was funny because the male lead (Donald Sutherland) was dressed in a corduroy suit and the female lead (not sure what her name is), was wearing a dress and high heels the entire time.

Anyway, being that I am always safety conscious, I commented on their attire and the fact that she was sprinting in high heels a little too well.

Now I know that there are a lot of you ladies out there that can do this but take heed. During the next chase scene, right after I made my comment, the female lead breaks her ankle because of her high heels.

Now...I'll admit I felt a little happy with my observation. Her ankle of course, ended up being her downfall as she got her 'Body Snatched' shortly thereafter because she couldn't run anymore.

As far as the corduroy suit...I'm not sure how that played into Donald's demise but rest assured, in the end, his body got snatched too!

Fashion vs. functional, you be the judge. And whatever you should decide, I'm pretty sure you should never wear corduroy.

If you want more Safety & Defense Tips...go to www.RealSafeDefense.com.

Edward T Aiken

CHAPTER 4

DO SMARTPHONES REALLY MAKE US ANY SMARTER?

Smartphones are the bane of most of our existences nowadays...aren't they. You can't go anywhere without seeing peoples faces glued to their tiny screens.

Yes...in ways they are sucking the life from us but you'd be hard pressed to find an agent nowadays who can do business without one. The fact is smartphones are here to stay.

I'll say it again...and probably again many times throughout this book but when it comes to your own personal safety, you have to analyze everything that you do. The things you do will either hinder your safety or help you to keep safe. What you do with the smartphone is no exception.

First, let's talk about the obvious. Texting is very necessary when it comes to business communication. Texting while driving ain't so smart but we all have done it, haven't we.

I"m sure you know that research has shown that texting while driving is more dangerous than drunk driving and I tend to agree. How many times have you seen a car in front of you weaving and when you get up next to them they've got their snout buried in their phone? Horrible.

In fact, here in Austin you can get a pretty hefty fine for texting as well as for talking on your phone while driving. It's okay if you use hands-free.

Now we can't even talk on the phone in one hand and drive. I blame the texters.

I'm actually not bringing this up because of texting/talking while driving but I am going to suggest a couple things when it comes to your safety while at your job.

In fact, I teach my self-defense students to do the same things I am going to teach you, when they are out in public.

The reason that texting while driving is so dangerous is the same reason why smartphones are destroying our social interactions.

That reason has to do with focus.

In order to use our smartphones we have to change our focus because of the size of the screens. This does a couple of things. It shuts off our peripheral vision which in turn creates tunnel vision. This in turn affects different parts of your brain. In other words it forces you to use different areas of your brain and those areas actually diminish your awareness of the outside world.

Sure, many of us can carry on a conversation and text, check our emails, etc. all at the same time, but it's not the same. Just ask my wife.

She yells at me every time I'm on the phone because I personally have a harder time listening to her. (A ploy I do not do on purpose...I swear.).

Of course if she wasn't always talking then that might not be a problem but that's a topic for a different book.

Let's get back to the focus thing. As a martial

arts instructor I would say that I am an expert on focus. When it comes to self-defense there are different types of focus, and the most important type of focus has to do with your visual acuity.

Our brains process the most information visually, provided you are not visually impaired of course. When a self-defense situation occurs, the more information you can process and the faster you can process it, the quicker you will respond and that increases your overall chances of survival.

Remember when Janice got attacked? Her attacker waited until she bent over and she was focused on the lock box when he struck her. He could have just as easily done this when she was checking her phone, couldn't he?

Focus and awareness go hand in hand.

So what do you do when you are expecting an important text, email, or phone call while with a client? We can't just shut off our business communications especially if it's crucial to your client's needs.

The answer I am going to give you is the same answer I give my self-defense clients.

When you are checking your email or texts, you need to hold the phone at eye level so that you can see both the phone and the client at the same time.

Don't worry, most people won't think twice about you holding the phone up to check your messages. Most people will just think you have bad eyesight or you are holding it that way because of the light. My eyesight sucks and I have to do it all the time.

When texting in public, I tell my self-defense clients to lean, stand, or sit with their back to a wall when possible and hold their phone up to eye level, I suggest you do the same thing. This way you can monitor your environment, including what's behind you.

The one thing about self defense is that danger can come from any direction and you have to monitor whats behind you as much as possible.

You can also check your messages/texts while walking but just know you are more open to attack from behind as opposed to standing with a wall at your back. In these cases I try to use reflective surfaces as much as possible to see what's behind me. It's a little awkward at first, but after a little practice it gets easier.

There's an app and device coming out soon that you might have seen.

It is for a hologram device for your car. What

it does is it projects your emails, texts, messages, onto the windshield so you don't have to take your eyes off the road.

This is similar to the HUD displays that fighter pilots use. Trust me...if the military does it, they've researched it and implement it because it works. Think about it...fighter pilots have to make quick decisions at high rates of speed, they can't afford to take their eyes off the horizon. The same goes for you.

Try it a few times and you'll see that it's actually easier to read your stuff too. Think...head up = alert. Head down = sleep and you can't afford to sleep on the job!

Now don't get me wrong...I do believe smartphones are not entirely useless when it comes to your safety. In fact they can mean the difference between life and death.

There are quite a few apps that have been developed to help with Realtor Safety. I personally haven't used them so I can't give a specific recommendation at this point.

I do know that there are apps that keep track of your location and you can enter who you are with, time of your appointments, etc. These are great and in the future I will research them more and give you my opinion. I think having a GPS app to report your location is critical. Hopefully,

I'll try some out soon but ultimately, YOU are your best bet.

One thing you can do also is to take some pictures of your new clients' license plate. I've done this in the past and usually just act like I'm taking a picture of the house.

You can even ask your clients if you can take a picture of them, if you haven't had the chance yet. Just tell them that you take pictures of all your clients and use them for marketing purposes. Most people won't have a problem with it. If they do there might be a good reason but this might also mean they have ulterior motives. Always be alert.

Of course your phone is also extremely important if you need to call for help. Beverly did the right thing and called her husband before her appointment to let him know where she'd be. Unfortunately she didn't get the chance to call for help once she needed it but that doesn't mean calling for help isn't important.

If you do get attacked and happen to get away one of the first things you should do, once you get a safe distance, is to call 911.

Distance first, 911 second. Remember armed help...ie the police are too far away and you can't depend on them to get to you in time but you should still call them when you can do so safely.

Your attacker may still be trying to get to you. Just make sure you have the proper distance before you use your phone.

There's another important piece in this strategy that often goes overlooked.

In order to call the police, guess what? Your phone has to have power. I am quite guilty of this and you might be too but let me ask you...how often does your phone run out on you while you are at work?

Always...always...always make sure that you have enough juice in your phone before an appointment. Always make sure you have a car charger...in fact I recommend having 2 since I've gone through multiple chargers myself as they seem to stop working after awhile. Keep your phone charged!

You should also have extra batteries handy. Once again, 2 is the magic number. Extra battery packs are pretty inexpensive nowadays. There are also larger portable battery packs that act like chargers, these are great too. I've got a few. They work great for camping.

The bottom line is that providence favors the prepared. Be the Boy Scout or Girl Scout of your office. Hone your awareness and supplement it with as many things as you can.

You know the other day I was joking with a client as I was putting his info in my phone...

I was reminiscing about the days when we had everybody's numbers memorized. In fact I still remember my friend Dan's home number from when I was 11 years old. Isn't that crazy?

But today, I'd have a difficult time remembering many of my friend's or family's numbers. I do know my wife's but that's really it and that's only because I needed to know it for the Pet Food Club Discount at the store.

Technology really can dumb us down. Perhaps that is the point of having it?

The lesson is to use technology wisely but don't put all of your reliance on it. Your own awareness is more important when it comes to your own safety.

So I implore you to please take an active approach to improving your own safety awareness and supplement them with technology. Rely on yourself over others, over technology, or even authority figures (the police) to keep you safe. This is the mindset that is needed in those critical dangerous moments I hope none of you ever have to face. You have to be self-reliant because at those moments, you are all alone.

On a final note I want to say that you should always strive to have your phone with you. Don't leave it at the car or at the office. Have it on you, charged, and ready to use.

Personally I would keep it in a pocket unless you are using it to take pictures or checking your messages. At least you should have it with you.

I know there are some safety trainers who say you should always have your phone in your hand when with clients...I disagree. We'll talk about what you should be carrying in your hands in a bit but for now, just make sure you can access it quickly in a time of need.

You never know when you might need to run out the back door and away from your car. You don't want to have to circle back to your car to get your phone and you don't want to be running into unknown parts of a neighborhood without a means of calling for help.

So what about the cases where you don't get a signal?

I say...be extra cautious for one. If you know beforehand that you don't get a signal at a particular property make sure you tell someone where you will be at, what your time frame is for being there, and the fact that there is no cell service out there. I would even make sure that you have that same person check on you after that time frame is up to make sure you are okay.

You don't necessarily have to be the victim of a violent crime to need help either.

A few years ago I had hurt my knee training in Jiu-Jitsu. I was just off crutches and had to go inspect a house. It was vacant and was on a sloped lot. I left my phone in my and wouldn't you know it...I fell as I stepped off a small ledge on the side of the house. It wasn't a big fall but my knee was still so damaged that it took me quite some time to make it back on my feet and back to the car.

The funny thing was I had hurt my knee on several previous occasions and was pretty familiar with the healing process as well as how badly it can affect one's mobility. I should have known better.

The second time I had hurt my knee over the years prior to the time I am sharing with you...I popped my knee out in my living room I ended up lying on my living room floor unable to move for quite some time. I couldn't reach my phone which was on the kitchen counter nor could I move around very well without excruciating pain. I ended up being sprawled on the floor for a good hour and a half before my landlady found me.

Luckily I lived in a guest house and the owner frequently worked on the plants in her yard each day which were outside my window, otherwise who knows how long I would have been there.

She helped me up to a set of crutches I kept in my closet. I kept those glued to my side thereafter.

Talk about feeling helpless. Had there been a 'Body Snatcher' there I most certainly would have been toast.

Well maybe not, my wonderful dog was there to console me with the occasional face lick so I wasn't completely alone. She probably would've protected me.

Aren't animals wonderful?

People on the other hand...are why I have to write this, unfortunately.

Anyway...it goes without saying, I should have known better than to look at a property, without my phone and without my crutches on a hurt knee but we all make mistakes. Please learn from mine.

Go get on my email list on my website and I'll be sure to post my review of some safety apps soon...

www.RealSafeDefense.com.

Edward T Aiken

CHAPTER 5

SPATIAL AWARENESS IS CRITICAL

Most people who don't actively train in self-defense don't really understand when or how an attacker will attack. That's okay for most people but in our industry it is crucial that you know.

You are in an industry where you have a 40% higher chance of becoming victimized by a violent crime while on the job than when compared to the national average. There are multiple reasons for this...

First...the majority of agents in real estate are female. That's not to say that men don't get attacked or robbed but the overwhelming victims of violent crimes who are in real estate are female.

One of the main reasons is that you ladies are targets of opportunity. You are often meeting strangers at remote locations...alone. Most of you have your picture as part of your advertising and your schedule can be found out pretty easily through the internet. We've already covered most of this but there are some other things I want you to start thinking about.

Other reasons crimes against Real Estate Agents are so high has to do with the physical nature of your job and that is the fact that you are often walking clients through a house. This gives a potential attacker plenty of time to observe you, how you move, how aware you are, and ultimately how easy of a target you might be.

Criminals are cowards who like to prey on people that they feel will give them the least amount of resistance. In fact, just today I saw a news article about a pregnant lady who got held up at Target here in town.

If you know anything about Austin, it is one of the safest cities to live in. Unfortunately we are growing exponentially and we are starting to experience the problems of bigger cities.

Anyway...some DirtBag decided to hold the poor woman up at gunpoint. She was with her 4 year old AND she was 8 months pregnant. This guy was pretty bold too. Apparently there was a witness standing nearby watching the whole thing. This guy didn't even care. He pulled his gun out and told the lady that he would shoot her daughter first and then kill her and her unborn child next.

Talk about a piece of trash.

I think most people will agree with that statement but I have to say...from a criminal's standpoint, he selected the perfect target. What parent in their right mind would ever risk their child's life or their unborn child's life for their wallet?

And if you're wondering...no I would not advocate this lady do anything to defend herself physically. The only time I would tell her that she needed to do something physical is if this guy tried to take her child or she knew beyond a shadow of a doubt that he was going to kill her or her child.

No...she did the right thing. She complied with him, gave him what he wanted, and he left. Some would say that this is a no win situation. I disagree.

This young mother won because she got to go home at night with her children and that's all that counts. Stuff is just stuff but life is beyond precious.

So let's get back to the theme of this

chapter...spatial relationship. What do I mean when I say spatial relationship?

When it comes to your personal safety while doing your job you have to constantly keep in mind where you are in relation to your client as well as where you are in relation to your nearest escape route.

I use the term escape route because your escape route doesn't always equate into the nearest exit. You may be towards the back of a house near the rear door when you get attacked but that doesn't mean the back door is your nearest escape exit. The backyard might be enclosed with high locked fences with no possible route to your car. The backyard/door in this instance will not be your nearest escape route.

So let's go over some things to do and think about as you are walking a client through a house and/or you are walking yourself through a vacant house when it comes to your escape route. First...hopefully you've already covered spatial relationship when it comes to parking your car and it's not blocked in.

This is the first part of your thinking when it comes to your escape route, your car. When you can...if things go bad, you want to get to your car and get out of there.

So let's extrapolate on this thought and start

with the beginning of a typical appointment.

When you get out of your car after you've parked it where you won't be blocked in, you need to have what the military calls 360 degree awareness. You need to observe what is behind you, to your left, your right, and in front of you. You need to be aware of your terrain and environment and not have your nose in your phone.

Are you on concrete, grass, or mud...Has it recently rained?

Are there any blind spots where someone might possibly be standing or hiding? Where is your client(s) in relation to you?

These are the things that you need to observe and think about as you are walking up to the door of the property.

Most of the time you will walk up to the door, find the lock box, pick it up, and get the key. Then you will insert the key and open the door. The only thing that's really different is how you are using your awareness and spatial relationship.

Remember...Janice and the lock box!

Opening the door to a property is THE MOST CRITICAL TIME for your safety. You are in a vulnerable position most of the time that it takes you to get the key out, put it in the lock, and open the door. Your focus is divided.

Often a criminal will take this opportunity to rush you from a hiding spot while you are busy opening the door, or walking towards the door. Sometimes they might even already be hiding in the house and attack as you open the door or like in Janice's case the client might attack you as you are accessing the lock box

One of the things I teach during the actual hands-on part of the REAL SAFE DEFENSE course is how to specifically preposition yourself so that you can both defend and escape using the path of least resistance.

For example...if you happen to be meeting a client at a property, you want to walk on the side that is the most open. Think of a house that has a garage where you need to walk around the side of the garage to get to the front door. You want to keep your client in between you and the wall while you are between the client and the open space. In other words if you are walking towards the front door and there is a wall on your right and an open yard to your left. Keep your client on the right and you stay left...closest to your escape route.

You do this so that your client has less of a chance to catch you and pin you against a wall and you have more area to run.

Every time you walk into a property with your client you have a choice...Do you walk in first or let your client go first? This can be an awkward decision given the social niceties can come into play.

How often have you stood there holding a door and the person insists you go first? After you...no after you...no, no I insist...After you! It can be tricky navigating this as you have to consider that this is the most opportune time for an attack. And not to mention that there might be someone on the other side of that door waiting for you.

What to do? What to do?

Luckily I have a pretty good answer for you unfortunately it is easier to show you than to explain but I'll do my best.

I call it the Curtsy Maneuver.

As you are opening the door to a property you want to make sure you are at a 45 degree angle to your client. Hopefully they are on the side of the wall but often will be standing back a little bit behind you. It's imperative to make sure you can see them the entire time. To do this effectively you want to to engage them in smalltalk as you are opening a door.

Engaging them in conversation will give you the excuse to slightly turn towards them as you are opening the door. This in turn will keep them in view as well as give you a good position to protect yourself should the need arise.

The Curtsy Maneuver goes like this...

As you open the door, take a step back at a 45 degree angle and gesture for them to go in first. You can even do a little curtsy as you slightly bow allowing them to go in. The step you take, takes you out of the path of the door giving them the right of way so to speak. It's easier for them to enter than you as they will then be closer.

If that's too awkward you can open the door first, just make sure to open it all the way as you step back. Don't follow the door to open it like we do most of the time. Swing it open, and tell them to go on in as you angle towards the lock box It will look like you are putting the key back or that you need to do something with the lock box prior to going in.

Btw...a lock box is an amazing weapon!

Once you enter the house behind them, make sure that before you step in that the door has been opened as far as it can. This is to insure that no one is standing behind it or to the side. Visually you want to scan the house quickly from left to right. As you step in turn slightly to look back outside to make sure no one is there.

The thing to look out for at this point is called a 'Pincer Move'. A group of really coordinated attackers would use this opportunity in time to take advantage of your position.

A Pincer Move works like this...

As you enter the property, an attacker would run from around the corner in the front door while at the same time the so-called client or other person runs at you from the opposite direction sandwiching you in the middle. Talk about being between a rock and a hard place.

No doubt...this situation is tough to deal with but not impossible. Of course the solution needs to be shown as it's too much to write about here. That's why we have the Real Safe Defense Program.

Now let's get back to your appointment.

Provided the above didn't happen and you are not trapped between 2 attackers, you now have another choice...do you shut the front door or leave it open.

Unfortunately there is not one answer. The real answer is that it depends on the entirety of that particular situation.

There are times you want the door open and times you want to have it shut. The one thing you don't want to do is to lock it behind you. Once again, it's important to role play through different scenarios so you can get comfortable with the different escape options available to you.

The complexities involved is why it's so important to get Realistic Self-Defense Training. I can not emphasize this enough.

Now back to the house...if you are in a house you haven't 'cleared' yet, you need to proceed with caution. Remember my story about appraising the house at the beginning of this book...there were 2 people in the house the whole time and I had no idea.

One of the next things I would do is unlock and open your secondary escape routes if you have them. It might be a rear door or a side door. I would open them all. Keep your client in sight as much as possible and be aware of where you are in relation to them and your escape routes.

Use caution and your senses as you walk into rooms you haven't been in yet. Watch and Listen for indications that there might be someone else in the house.

If you really want to be safe let your client walk through the house on their own and stay near the front door with it open, so you can see outside and inside at the same time.

Let's say this isn't the case and you decide to proceed through the house with your clients. What do you do when it comes to stairs?

The rule for stairs is pretty standard.

Always let your client go ahead of you. There are some areas of concern that will depend on where you are in relation to your client.

If you are walking UP the stairs behind your client be aware that your face is often in line with their feet and you are in the perfect position for them to turn around to kick you in the face or even to back kick you in the face. To make sure they can't do this just make sure you have enough distance, it's pretty easy to judge.

Conversely, in those instances where it's not possible to let your client go first, then know you are in a good position to kick them in the face. Just keep them in the proper striking distance.

The thing to watch out for when you are walking in front of them is that they don't reach out and grab your feet to pull you down the stairs. This is a pretty common move during domestic assaults btw.

On the way down I would say that it is

imperative that you let them go first or you go at a time when they aren't behind you. A dubious attacker knows that pushing you from behind down a flight of stairs is a quick, easy way to incapacitate you and to make it look like an accident.

Let them go first. The thing to look for is the foot grab only know they have to turn around to do it. If this happens grab the railing (you should be already) and kick them as hard as you can. If you have enough space between you and them, they won't be able to grab you.

And...never go into the basement. Bad things always happen in basements.

Ultimately, using proper spatial relationship requires a little bit of practice and knowledge of what can happen.

It will take a bit of conscious thought in the beginning to get good at it, but once you've gone through a good defense course that addresses this issue, you will be 1000 times more prepared than if you've never thought about it before.

Further, the habit of having spatial relationship awareness will transfer over to an overall sense of awareness of your environment no matter where you are at.

Before you know it, you will find yourself

positioning in the best way for your own safety at the coffee shop, at the grocery store, getting gas...practically everywhere.

Edward T Aiken

**To get started on your Awareness Training
go to...**

www.RealSafeDefense.com.

CHAPTER 6

STARTING WITH YOUR FIGHT & FLIGHT PLAN!

Now it's time to start to put together some strategies to deal with your Fight & Flight or just a Flight plan.

Remember your first priority is to Escape Safely.

You may or may not have to Fight in order to escape but if you do need to, you have to have a solid strategy and some experience (ie...practice) in order to know how you will most likely respond under duress.

The biggest drawback when it comes to physically defending oneself...is that a lot of people think they already know how they will react once a defensive situation occurs. A lot of that is ego and a lot of that is simply watching too many kung fu movies as a kid.

I can't tell you how many people have told me that they aren't worried how they will handle themselves because they'll just 'kill someone'. They usually say something along the lines of...I grew up with brothers, I've got quite a temper, I got in fights when I was younger, I train cross-fit...etc.

Well that's all fine and good and you MAY be right but most of the time I've found that the rigid rod of reality is just plain hard and when it hits you it hits you HARD.

In my experience people do one of four or five things when they are confronted with violence.

Some will instantly get scared, their adrenaline will kick in, and they will haul ass. Nothing wrong with that but you don't want to rely on it because whose to say that the criminal won't be faster than you.

Some will instantly freeze. They immediately go into shock and just freeze. Their system just shuts down and they are unable to act. Often they will follow the instructions of the attacker but will find it difficult to move as they shake in fear. I've had this response before and it's not fun. With training you can overcome it.

Some will try to reason their way out of the situation. This isn't all that bad of a strategy. If you can get away with it and it avoids violence, by all means use it...but it doesn't always work and can in fact work against you.

It worked for Janice. Once she was hit, she didn't fight or run but instead...asked her attacker why he hit her. Janice was a former airline attendant and was trained to remain calm. She managed to talk to her attacker for 45 minutes until she found her opportunity to escape. To me...the ability to use Verbal Judo is just as important as using real Judo. You never know how long your verbal judo is going to work or when you might need to go to the physical. Sometimes you can simply use reasoning to end it and sometimes not.

Others will get angry and Fight...Ineffectively. We all have a Fight or Flight response in us and depending on the situation one or the other can kick it in. Most of the people who choose to fight usually do so ineffectively. This is due to too much raw emotion and too little training. Once again...with the right training one can learn to minimize their responses to their emotions and fight (defend themselves) in an effective manner.

Finally there are those that will Fight...Effectively. These people are the minority.

There is a certain percentage of the population who are natural fighters and are just plain tough. The problem is that criminals are usually pretty good at avoiding these types of people. Remember, most criminals are going to scout you out beforehand. If they perceive that you are going to be a problem they will most likely move on to some lower hanging fruit. The thing is to make sure you're not deluding yourself into thinking you fall into this category.

And if you can fight it's still good to have proper training and a plan.

The biggest thing you need to do is to uncover which response(s) you are most likely to have and to work on being able to do whichever one the situation at hand calls for (minus the fighting ineffectively response of course.)

The way to do this is obviously with a trained self-defense expert who can not only teach you the moves but can show you how to cultivate the right responses.

If you don't have the opportunity to train with someone right away, having the right strategy in place is a good place to start. We've already covered most of it so far, but it is a good idea to start thinking about applying these strategies in real situations so that you have a realistic idea of what to do and how you're going to respond.

We already know that the overall goal is to Escape safely. So let's talk about some options that we might use in case violence actually occurs. Here's brief list (in no particular order of importance) of what we might do if attacked...

Run away right away, reason with and persuade your opponent to let you go then run away, reason with your opponent and then run away when they are distracted, distract your opponent and run away, reason with your opponent – then strike them – then run away, strike your opponent right away and run away, or distract your opponent – strike them – and then run away, defend their attack and run away, etc...

See a pattern here? Everything ends with you running away...and escaping safely.

The trick is in knowing How Specifically to persuade, reason, distract, or strike them in order to get away safely. If you happen to strike an attacker with insufficient force then you might make the situation worse. You've got to stun them enough so that you can get away.

You also have to make sure that you take the proper escape route. It would do you little good to stun an attacker only to run into the backyard which has a 10 foot high fence with a locked gate!

When you start to really investigate what it might take to properly defense yourself you are most likely going to have questions.

For example...what should you be carrying in your hands. What shouldn't you be carrying. What about weapons? What about carrying a gun, a knife, or pepper spray? How do you strike them? Should you punch them? What if you break your hand? How are you going to sufficiently strike them if they are a lot bigger and stronger than you? What if they grab you?

We'll answer some of these questions in the next chapter but I want you to start realistically thinking about applying the strategies I've laid out for you so far. If you have any questions...write them down. The whole idea is to get you to start thinking with a proactive self-defensive mindset. Have a plan and train the plan. You're at the beginning of the plan. Awareness is a habit of thinking...a mindset that can keep you alive. It's not paranoia...it's preparation.

So...go through a few scenarios in you mind right now. Imagine if you were walking up to a vacant house with a new client and they grab you...what do you do? Go through the list. You can imagine striking them and running...reasoning with them and running...etc.

Do it now and I'll see you in the next chapter.

If you want more Resources on Planning for Safety...go to www.RealSafeDefense.com.

CHAPTER 7

SETTING UP FOR SURVIVAL

So far I've been giving you some strategies, ideas, and concepts when it comes to improving your overall self-defense. Now I want to dig a little deeper.

Those of you who decide to take this as deadly serious as you should are going to be much more prepared for a bad scenario to happen than those of you who are just reading this but don't put anything into action. That's of course true for just about anything but...this is an area that literally could mean the difference between life and death. Specifically...Your Life and Your Death!

I know that can sound a little harsh but that's the stone cold truth. Those of you that take the time to create and implement a new set of procedures and awareness at work will at the very least feel a little more secure because you are more prepared.

We've already talked about some things you can do a little differently when it comes to meeting new clients, walking them through houses, etc. Now I'm going to challenge you to start to put together your overall safety plan. I still have more to share with you as far as self-defense tips and strategies go, but I believe you have enough now to get the wheels turning.

So where do you start? First, let's take a quick look at some of the requirements of your job that are the most likely to get you into trouble.

Meeting and working with new clients is one of those areas. Many real estate offices will already have some policies in place concerning safety when dealing with new clients. Some of those policies will realistically help you while others may not. It is your job to figure out those procedures which will work for you specifically and which will not. Remember you have to balance your safety with your bottom line.

I know there are some offices out there that are a real pain to work at and have little regard for your own personal safety as they are concerned only with turning a profit. I'm also certain that they are the minority in the industry. But, if you do happen to be in an office that you feel is putting your safety second...leave. There are plenty of other places to hang your license. With that said let's get back to meeting and working with new clients.

What I want you to do is write out the preferred safety procedures you are to follow when meeting with a new client for the first time. Ideally, you will want to meet these clients at your office, with other people present, photocopy their id, and have them fill out a client form. Now...the key words here are preferred since this won't always be an option.

I want you to also write out a set of safety guidelines to follow for those times when you aren't with other people and are in the office alone or meeting them at some other location.

Here is what I suggest...

If you have to meet with a new client alone for the first time make sure to get at least their name and some other corresponding info like who referred them, etc. This may or may not be verifiable but every cop will tell you that every bit of information is valuable.

Once you have their name make sure you

coordinate with someone outside of the office...this can be another agent, a family member, or a friend. Give them the information and let them know what time you are meeting them. Make sure to set up a time for you to follow up with them and/or a time for them to follow up with you. In the event that you can't be reached by a certain time...have them call the proper authorities.

This type of procedure can work even if you are not meeting at the office. One thing I suggest is that your office has a set of codewords to indicate trouble. These code words are set up in the event that your perpetrator wants you to call someone to check in so they can have more 'time' with you. Once you call the office and give the appropriate code word...the person on the other end is to call the police immediately and give them all the other information that you have collected on the individual(s) you are meeting with, including your location, etc. Of course you can have different codewords for different scenarios but mainly they will be for emergencies only.

The next type of plan I want you to write out is a plan of what to do if you are showing a vacant house to new clients.

If a client wants to see a vacant house the best thing to do is simply open the door for them and let them tour the house on their own. Always keep in mind that someone else might be in that house. That person may or may not be in cahoots with your client. And don't worry about escorting your client, it's not your job to keep your client safe. You can answer any questions they have once they've looked through the house. Your safety comes first. If they ask you to 'come here and look at this', do so with caution.

You can also let them know that the house is vacant and that you haven't walked through it yet so 'please proceed with caution as you look through it.'

Write this as part of your plan as well as your procedures of how to let your office or someone helping you know when, where, and with whom you are meeting as well as what to do should you not check in by your predetermined time.

Next...as part of your overall procedures I would put in there something about only driving your own car and always having clients follow you in their own vehicle.

Many abductions have taken place because an agent let one of his/her clients talk them into riding with them in the agent's car while showing properties. I know there are some of you out there who use the opportunity of going from house to house together in a car as a time to further sell your clients...but I would suggest you don't need to.

If you have a client that is really adamant about riding with you...decline nicely and blame it on your office. Simply tell them that your broker's insurance doesn't cover them in the event someone were to hit you while you are driving them around even if it's not your fault. If they get mad at this, it should raise a red flag. It's best to just drop these types of clients anyways.

Another area of the job where agents have been victimized is at open houses. We've gone over this a little bit already but make sure to write out your procedures here as well.

Make sure to write out what to do if you have to show a house alone and with others. Who will be your contact to check in with...how will you check in...at what frequency...and what do they do should you fail to check in properly.

So far...you should have procedures for when you are meeting clients at the office both with others there and by yourself. You should also have your procedures for when you are meeting new clients in the field both with an assistant and alone. Make sure you include procedures for showing vacant houses and for sitting at open houses.

I also want you to write out procedures of what to do when you are staging a house or prepping a vacant house alone. These are for cases where you aren't with a client but you are also alone in a house. If you have to be in a house for awhile because you are getting it ready for prospective buyers...what are your procedures? What steps are you going to take to make sure you stay as safe as possible while you are busy prepping the house?

In times where you are prepping a house along, I would suggest that you keep all the doors and windows closed while you are decorating/staging and perhaps locked. This is done only after you have made sure no one else is in the house. Once the house is clear you can lock the doors/windows to make sure no one can sneak in while you are doing your work.

The rest of the plan is similar to what you've already done. Who are you to check in with and how, how often...etc.

Once you have written everything I have just gone over, also want you to write out a set of general safety tips and protocols to follow.

These are in no particular order and are more general in nature.

Here are some of the more general tips I want you to follow (feel free to add any I've overlooked):

Dress. Make sure to dress for the weather

and for functionality. If you have to escape make sure what you are wearing doesn't hinder you. Have the right clothes and shoes for the right weather and make sure they don't restrict your movement too much.

Jewelry. My advice is to tone it down. Many agents have been robbed because their perpetrators liked their jewelry. Keep your flashy jewelry at home or locked in your car hidden away from sight.

Phone. Charged at all times with extra batteries and chargers in your car. Keep your phone on you and accessible at all times.

Car. Gas at least ¾ of a tank full. Make sure the tires are good and there are no mechanical problems. Make sure to change your oil as scheduled as well.

Keys to Car. Have your keys on you at all times and accessible. If you have a wireless key chain make sure the battery works.

Purse. Keep it in the car and out of sight.

Self-Defense Item. We will cover this in an upcoming chapter.

Marketing Items. Prepare these ahead of time and keep them in a way that will enable you to carry them easily (more on this upcoming as well).

Additional Technology. Safety apps, GPS, etc. Make sure if you are on a subscription service that your service is active and functioning.

For More Safety Tips & Strategies go to my website www.RealSafeDefense.com.

Edward T Aiken

CHAPTER 8

THE SKINNY ON EXPERIENCING VIOLENCE WHILE ON THE JOB

After the last chapter, you should have a pretty solid set of safety guidelines and procedures to follow. Also, you should have an idea of the types of scenarios you are likely to encounter and some idea of what your responses should be such as distracting, striking, and escaping...etc.

We're going to go into more detail with the self-defense aspect now. The thing I want you to know is that no amount of explaining is satisfactory. Sure it helps...but there is no replacement for hands-on self-defense training. I can't emphasize this enough. I'll get into the types of training I recommend shortly but a good rule of thumb is that some training is better than no training at all.

In an ideal world, your awareness and safety procedures would be enough to keep you safe. In fact I would say that they will be enough for the majority of you. Sadly though...there will be some of you who no matter what you do or how safe you are you will inevitably come face to face with violence while at your job and it's my job to prepare you for it specifically.

So...let's talk about the reasoning why criminals might target you. It's important in the overall scheme of things to know the motivations of your perpetrators so you can best prepare your defenses.

In Real Estate, women are slightly more likely to get victimized on the job then men are...but not by much. Women are 57% likely while men are 43% likely to experience violence on the job.

I would say that the reason women have a greater chance to be victimized is because the criminals that prey on women have more 'reasons' to attack them.

If a man is attacked while on the job usually it is because of these motives:

Robbery...the perpetrators simply want to deprive them of their property. They may target them to steal their wallets, jewelry, items in the house, or their car.

The next reason is Assault...sometimes this is personal and sometimes it's not. Men will often get targeted for Assault where, for some reason, the perpetrator intends on doing harm to them. Often...assaults will occur in conjunction with robbery. Indeed, as we go through the list any one or more motives/criminal actions can happen during a crime.

Murder...men will often be targeted for murder. As with assault sometimes it's personal and sometimes not. Often, this happens in high crime areas but can happen anywhere.

Revenge...sometimes men are targeted (either with murder, or assault, or even false accusations/police charges) because a former client blames them for their shortcomings which were the result of a real estate deal. This often happens when a previous client loses their home due to foreclosure. They will blame everyone but themselves (a common criminal trait).

Now let's get to women. Women have all the above mentioned risk factors plus one or two more. Women can be targeted for Assault, Murder, Robbery, and Revenge just like men.

But...they also are targets of Sexual Crimes. Rape...sodomy...forced sexual acts...etc. Now, don't get me wrong...men have and do get raped but it's a very small percentage in our industry when compared to women.

As part of your business...you will often put our pictures, head shots, and glamor shots, on your advertising. Not all of you of course but it is a very common practice.

If your pictures happen to catch the eye of a sexual predator it can definitely lead to trouble. I'm not saying not to use glam shots in your advertising...but I would tone it down a bit especially if you feel some of your photos might be 'suggestive'. If you're not sure if they are suggestive, just ask people who you know you. I'm sure most of them will give you an honest opinion.

In real estate, I've seen some pretty 'sexed' up photos in LA. I'm not judging...sex sells and part of your job is to look good and professional. Just know the risks that go along with it. In fact...

A few years ago there was a young woman who had recently come here from Brazil. She had just gotten into Real Estate and had put up some photos with her ads.

Now to be honest, her real estate photos

weren't all that risky, but she did show some cleavage. The problem was that in addition to her ads, she had some pretty revealing bikini photos on her Facebook account which anyone could find by just Googling her name and occupation.

This girl had recently gotten implants and was proud of the way she looked. (Nothing wrong with that in my opinion unless of course you are talking about safety). Remember when in comes to safety you have to scrutinize everything you do especially if you are female.

Well as you can guess she caught the eye of a sexual predator. He contacted her and began communicating with her through Facebook. Now, he didn't exactly portray himself as someone in Real Estate but the lesson here is just as valid.

After exchanging some information, this guy found out where she lived and he ended up murdering her quite gruesomely.

I can't quite remember if he sexually assaulted her or not but I don't think it really matters. There are people in our society that live by different rules than we do and we have to realize that no amount of reasoning with them will help if they have their minds set on doing us harm.

All we can do is be diligent and prepare for the worst...How you can do that that specifically on the job is what we'll explore in the next chapter.

In the meantime...go to my website if you haven't done so yet and get on my mailing list to get some more valuable self-defense information.

Go now to www.RealSafeDefense.com.

102

CHAPTER 9

GUNS, KNIVES, PEPPER SPRAY...OH MY!

Now it's time to talk about what you can do physically to Even the Odds!   Remember, a criminal who has targeted you already has the advantage because they already know what they are going to do whereas you have to react to what they do.   Action is always faster than reaction.

If you have ever taken the time to look at the reality of how violent things actually occur in the real world, you know that it isn't pretty.

As part of wanting to give my students access to the best possible information out there...I have spent hundreds of hours researching, watching, and dissecting all sorts of violent videos.

Some of it is too brutal even for me to watch but I try to force my way through it because it's imperative to my students' safety. I know (from personal experience) what can happen and just how bad something can get in the blink of an eye and I also know how unpredictable violence can be.

Through looking and experiencing just how violence can occur and experimenting and refining an answer for it, I've developed a few opinions on how I think that should be done which I'm going to share with you. Just bear in mind that these are my opinions and other self-defense instructors have their own. As far as you are concerned, the more information on this topic that you get, the better.

So...let's look at some of the self-defense options available to you.

As part of my approach, I am of the opinion that you as a real estate agent need to carry an equalizer...a self-defense item that will help to even the disadvantage. Most of you won't have the luxury of time to train in all sorts of disciplines so you can develop a high level of skill. So...you need something simple, effective, easy to learn and that can even the odds as much as possible.

Now, I live here in Texas and we're kind of partial to our guns. You may or may not like firearms. Whatever your beliefs on them are, that's fine, I'm just going to share a little bit about mine.

As part of my company, I teach close-quarter handgun training and think it's a valuable skill that everyone needs to have especially in today's world. A handgun is one of the absolute best self-defense weapons available but only with the proper training.

So...let's look at carrying a gun while on the job. You may even already have your permit and carry one now.

First, in my opinion, if you are going to carry a firearm you are going to need more than just the requirements that you will need to get your license to carry one. It's fairly easy to get your Concealed Handgun License. All you have to do is pass a safety class, fire a few rounds at a range, and then you get your Concealed Handgun License in the mail. Of course you have to pass a background check too.

The problem is that the requirements to get your license teach you very little, if anything, that will prepare you to handle your gun in a life and death situation.

Imagine if someone were to attack you out of the blue at work. They jump out from behind a bush and start punching you. What do you do? Most people would say that they would just pull out their gun and Bam...that's it.

Well...I'm here to tell you that once someone has punched you and is punching, pushing, kicking, and pulling you it is extremely difficult to grab your gun from your pocket, waistband, or purse (unless of course you have already practiced and prepared for that in what we call a Force on Force Training Class). Otherwise, you will have no balance and will most likely be disoriented from the strikes. Violence happens fast and is very confusing and shocking.

Many women carry their guns in their purses. How are you going to get your gun out of your purse if it is flying everywhere, has been grabbed, or is on the ground as a result of the ongoing onslaught you are experiencing? What if your gun falls out of your purse and the attacker grabs it?

Accessing your gun in the heat of a struggle is not as easy as people think.

The bottom line is you have to have the proper training, where you are practicing drawing, retention, muzzle awareness, and shooting all while under pressure and duress AND this type of training has to be done with the utmost of safety.

If you don't have access to that type of training I would suggest you pass on carrying a gun for now. As part of my company, like I said, I do do this type of training but it is more of a follow-up to our Real Safe Defense Course but I will say that our Real Safe Defense Course helps set you up for our Handgun Course. The moves are designed so you can follow up and access your handgun the proper way.

It is worth noting that here in Texas it is legal even without a license, to carry a loaded gun in your car. As long as you know proper firearm safety and are familiar with your handgun, I do recommend keeping it in your car. If you are attacked and you are able to escape to your car, then you should have time to get your gun out once the door is locked.

So as far as carrying one on your person...a gun is out until you get the proper training.

The next best weapon in my opinion, is a knife. Now, once again you are going to have similar problems as you had with the gun. Since you aren't going to be walking around showing a house to a client with your knife in your hand, you will still have to access it in heat of the moment.

Fighting with a knife is one of my specialties. I have thousands of hours of knife training along with hundreds of hours of actually watching video on real stabbings, robberies with a knife, knife attacks, etc. and my conclusion is that a knife for the average real estate agent is a bad idea.

First, it is a very gruesome thing and most people don't have the stomach to stab or slash someone.

Second, the person with the knife often ends up cutting themselves in some fashion. The last thing we want to do is take additional damage.

Third, unless you hit the proper areas, a knife might not stop the attacker as it can take a while for them to slow down and bleed out. People can keep fighting for quite some time if a knife has not pierced a major organ or artery.

Finally, because it's a knife, it can escalate things. In other words if your attacker was just trying to scare you into giving up your jewelry and you slash him with a knife...if he doesn't run he will most likely try to kill you. He might do this if you strike him too but an attacker is more likely to escalate things once a knife comes out. Knives...psychologically, are for intimidation and killing and criminals know this.

So...the knife is out. Unless of course you get the proper training which takes time.

Now the next self-defense items aren't really items I consider to be necessarily good for self-defense but they are commonly marketed to real estate agents so I'll cover them here.

Pepper spray. I know that some of you have

pepper spray on your key chain right now, and some of you even carry it in your hand while you are showing houses. This is not a bad idea but it's not the best.

There are a couple of problems when it comes to pepper spray.

First, it doesn't always work. Depending on the quality of the brand and the resistance of your attacker to it, it can often times be ineffective.

Second, you have to access it and point it in the right direction under stress. Sure you might have it in your hand dangling on your key chain but you still have to make sure you are pointing it the right way once you grab it?

What if you accidentally spray yourself?

And...even if you have your pepper spray pointed in the right direction, it still might blow back in your face.

What if you get back to your car only to have the effects hit you and you end up being too blind to drive away safely?

I'm not saying pepper spray can't work...practically all self-defense items can and do work at the right times, but you have to consider the risk to reward ratio and with pepper spray I'm just not convinced.

Finally, the last one is the taser.

Unfortunately, most of the tasers available to the public aren't all that effective. They don't have a strong enough jolt. It has to do with the amperage and not the voltage.

The cops have the good tasers and they do work very well but you have to make sure you are getting what they get and most people don't know the difference.

Then, even if you do have a good taser, the problem once again has to do with accessing it under duress.

The tasers that cops have also fire like guns so you can hit a person at a distance as well as can be used up close. We civilians have access to those too but mostly we are marketed the ones that you have to use up close and most of the popular ones have high voltage but not enough amperage to stop an attacker. Don't worry too much about the science.

Bottom line is you're not going to be walking a client around with a taser in your hand. If you did you probably wouldn't keep too many clients that way. So we are back to the accessing problem and that means tasers are out.

At the beginning of this chapter I stated that I

believe you need to carry an equalizer (a self-defense item) in addition to empty-hands training...so what do I recommend if you can't use any of the items I've just listed?

Obviously I'm going to share that with you (in the next chapter), but I want to reiterate the points and problems that I've gone over in this chapter when it comes to using self-defense tools.

One of the biggest thing has to do with accessing your weapon under stress. If someone is going to attack you and you don't catch their intentions beforehand,...you are going to have to play catch up.

Being one step behind in a life and death struggle because you have to get your equalizer out is not some place you want to be...BUT that doesn't mean you can't prepare for it.

You always want to prepare for the worst. The idea of course, is to give you all the tools possible to hedge the advantage back into your favor. Accessing a weapon during a real attack takes time and training. We need something that is effective, simple, and doesn't take that much training to implement.

So if we ARE going to use an equalizer then it is going to have to be something we don't have to access...and our attacker doesn't think all that much about it.

In other words, it has to be something we can carry in our hand while we are with our clients and that item doesn't alarm them. It also has to be effective, easy to use, and work in conjunction with our hand to hand training.

And that self-defense tool is...a Tactical Pen.

If you want more Resources on Self Defense Items...go to www.RealSafeDefense.com

CHAPTER 10

THE TACTICAL PEN!
A REALTOR'S BEST FRIEND...

So...what is a Tactical Pen?

A tactical pen is a specially designed pen made of a hard material (usually metal) that has a sharp point at one or both ends. It is made of reinforced material that you can use the points either as an impact weapon or as a glass-breaker in the event of an emergency. It is tough, durable, and effective.

Tactical pens come in all shapes and sizes and can range in price from $5 to $500. The pens I recommend are actually on the cheaper side. They work just as well as the more expensive ones and are a little larger than some of the other pens out there.

I'll admit, the size and look can be a little intimidating but if you carry it the way I teach you to in the Real Safe Defense Course...your clients will never notice.

In fact, I demonstrate this point when I do presentations on Safety at Real Estate Offices. I have a pen in my hand the entire time and at the end of the presentation I ask if anyone noticed anything 'special' or different about the pen I was holding. No one ever does.

Here is a picture of the ones I am currently recommending and that I give to you when you take our full Real Safe Defense course.

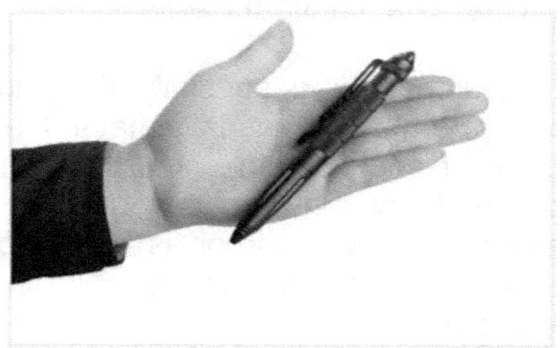

As you can see the pen is pretty robust but trust me, your clients, even the ones with ill intentions will not notice if you carry it correctly.

Now, I want you to think about 'why' the Tactical Pen is perfect for your line of work.

It's not unusual for an agent to have a pen in their hand especially if you are using it to circle certain items on the MLS, brochures, etc.

When you use it as a pointer it is even less conspicuous as it becomes part of your presentation style, like when I give my presentations. You simply use it to point out different features of the house you are showing.

There are some drawbacks to these pens...and that is that the ink runs out pretty quickly and you have to order the ink cartridges through Amazon but that is really a minor thing when compared to their functionality as a self-defense tool.

Also, the tactical pens won't necessarily take an aggressive attacker out of commission permanently like a gun but they can and will effectively stun them long enough for you to follow-up with something that will allow you to escape.

The reason the Tactical Pen is a good stunning tool is because of the sharp point and hardness of the material, they inflict quite a bit of pain when you strike the right areas.

Inflicting this 'moment of pain' will temporarily pattern interrupt their system and that in turn will allow you to then hit them with one of your heavier strikes (which we teach), which will stun them long enough for you to escape.

In the Real Safe Defense Course we teach you how to properly grip the pen and we show you how to strike with it from different angles.

We show you how to use it to defend against different types of attacks like bear hugs, chokes, holds, and strikes. We also show you how to use it if you get knocked to the ground.

In the Real Safe Defense Course, you will also learn not only different types of strikes you can do with the tactical pen, but what areas to strike which will inflict the most pain on your opponent.

All of this of course, is in addition to your empty-hands training. You have to be able to defend yourself first and foremost when you are unarmed. Unless you're going to carry your pen with you 24/7, you should make sure your empty-hands self-defense is functional, effective, and simple.

A good self-defense program will cover many different scenarios and should give you a variety of simple yet effective options. I emphasize simple and effective because in the heat of the moment you don't want to have to recall some complicated move.

Any program worth it's salt should teach you how to defend against strikes, grabs, throws, chokes, from the front, back, sides, and all of the above from different positions on the ground.

You also never want to overlook the ground because chances are pretty high that you will either trip or get knocked down so it's important to know how to defend yourself while you're down there as well as how to get up the proper way so you can escape safely.

A good self defense program also has to have some sort of realism involved in its training and that means there has to be some stress and some pressure. You can't just do moves on your coworkers while they just stand there.

It doesn't mean you should get hurt doing the techniques but there should be some drills to ensure that you are experiencing a good deal of stress and pressure. Otherwise you will never know how well you will perform when/if it ever happens to you for real.

The other things that a good self-defense program should offer is what we've already covered in this book and that is awareness, escape, and safety strategies.

At the risk of sounding like a shameless self-promoter, I have to say that I am pretty proud of the Real Safe Defense Program.

I think that not only does the Real Safe Defense Program have the best information as far as self-defense goes, but it is tailor-made for your job.

I am uniquely aware of how Real Estate Professionals need to do their job and I know how some of the safety guidelines you have been previously taught can be hard to stick to when you are out there trying to service your clients.

The truth is most of you are going to meet clients at vacant and remote locations at some point. You are going to be at vacant homes alone at others. And some of you are even going to to roll the dice and let a new client ride in the car with you. And despite all this...most of you will never experience any problems whatsoever.

But...no matter what we do bad things are going to happen to good people and I'm of the opinion that they shouldn't happen to you.

**So if you haven't yet, go to
www.RealSafeDefense.com
and sign up for one of our courses.**

**I promise you will not be disappointed and
if you are for some crazy reason...I'll let
you keep the pen.**

Edward T Aiken

CONCLUSION...

My hope for you is that this book acted as a primer to improve your overall safety awareness and to give you some options to do that effectively.

I know without a doubt that this material is some of the best...if not THE BEST available and I hope you will take advantage of it. The last thing anyone wants to see is a repeat of the tragedies we experienced in the recent years. If this book helps to prevent that then I am happy.

I'd like to part with a story if I may...

Years ago before I was in Real Estate, I had a student who had previously been raped and came to me wanting to learn to protect herself. As you can imagine the ordeal she went through was horrible but she was a strong willed person and was determined to work through it. The problem was she was having Post Traumatic Stress and found it hard to be around people. She couldn't work and was pretty depressed. It took a lot of guts to come to a man for help.

At that time I had a martial arts school and I agreed to teach her several times during the week in the morning. As part of the training I had to ask her how the attack happened not only so that I could prepare her in case it ever happened again, but also so that I could help her work on getting over her previous attack in her mind. I made it more about how he physically did it and didn't delve too much into the other details. I would often attack her in the exact same manner that led to her getting raped and you could see it really affected her.

Anyway, I trained her 3-4 times a week for a couple months and the training was always geared towards her defending herself in various ways and getting away. She got so good at it that I would actually test her by just attacking her in mid-conversation and before I knew it she would was out the door.

After a couple months I decided to move back to California (my school was in Michigan), to continue my training. The school was doing well but I wasn't too happy with the arrangement I had with my partners so I left.

Anyway...I found out that a few months after I left, that the person that had attacked my student had tried to do it again. I never realized that he was still out there, for some reason I assumed he had been caught but in reality he never was.

In retrospect, this made me really admire my student even more because not only did she have to deal with the trauma of the attack but she had to deal with the stress caused by not knowing who this guy was or if he would try to do it again.

Well what I gathered was that this guy thought he would give it another go. He broke into her house when she wasn't there and waited for her in her bedroom. She walked into the bedroom and apparently as he jumped out to grab her she unleashed a barrage of knees to his groin, gouged his eyes, and elbowed him several times. I say apparently because my student didn't quite remember how it transpired. She said she reacted on pure instinct and muscle memory. In essence she did exactly as I drilled her to do and before she knew it she was out the door and down the street at a neighbors house who she knew.

They called the police immediately and they arrived within a few minutes of the assault. The guy tried to get away but didn't get very far because he was having a hard time walking. They found him a few yards from her back door clutching his crushed testicles.

I share this story not only because it makes me feel good that I had some sort of hand in stopping a rapist, but in also helping to take out his weapon of choice!   Ha...

But with all kidding aside my student went back to her job shortly after that and eventually got married.   This to me is the real reason I do what I do.   I know bad things like this do happen and will happen again but I also now know that not only can they be prevented from happening again but that even if they do, a person can at least gain back some of that which has been unjustly taken from them.

And as far as you're concerned, let's make it so that you don't lose anything...ever.   Thank You...and God Bless!

ABOUT THE AUTHOR

Edward T. Aiken is a Certified Residential Appraiser, a First Degree Black Belt in Brazilian Jiu Jitsu, and a Full Instructor in Jeet Kune Do Concepts. Mr. Aiken divides his time between Appraising and Teaching, Training, and Coaching Groups, Individuals, and Professional Athletes in Self-Defense, Mixed Martial Arts, and Brazilian Jiu-Jitsu. Mr. Aiken is also a Keynote Speaker and has been featured at numerous conventions, podcasts, and seminars. Mr. Aiken's current programs can be found at:

Fight Fast 'n Flee
(www.FightFastnFlee.com)
Real Safe Defense
(www.RealSafeDefense.com)
Experts Training Academy
(www.ExpertsTrainingAcademy.com)